For J.burl, Jaims, Bianks, Sof, Daddy Ed, Mommy Tess, Dad Nards,
Mom Kay and the rest of my wonderful family — GRJ

With love to Beti, Chloe, Ziggy, Xylo, Sophie, Lei, Elijah and Sam,
grandnephews and grandnieces around the globe — CDA

All About the
PHILIPPINES

Stories, Songs, Crafts
and Games for Kids

GIDGET ROCELES JIMENEZ

Illustrated by

CORAZON DANDAN-ALBANO

TUTTLE Publishing

Tokyo | Rutland, Vermont | Singapore

"Books to Span the East and West"

Tuttle Publishing was founded in 1832 in the small New England town of Rutland, Vermont (USA). Our core values remain as strong today as they were then—to publish best-in-class books which bring people together one page at a time. In 1948, we established a publishing office in Japan—and Tuttle is now a leader in publishing English-language books about the arts, languages and cultures of Asia. The world has become a much smaller place today and Asia's economic and cultural influence has grown. Yet the need for meaningful dialogue and information about this diverse region has never been greater. Over the past seven decades, Tuttle has published thousands of books on subjects ranging from martial arts and paper crafts to language learning and literature— and our talented authors, illustrators, designers and photographers have won many prestigious awards. We welcome you to explore the wealth of information available on Asia at www.tuttlepublishing.com.

Published by Tuttle Publishing, an imprint of Periplus Editions (HK) Ltd.

www.tuttlepublishing.com

Library of Congress Cataloging-in-Publication Data
Jimenez, Gidget, 1964- author.
All about the Philippines : stories, songs, crafts and games for kids / Gidget Jimenez ; illustrated by Corazon Dandan-Albano.
   63 pages : illustrations, maps ; 29 cm
ISBN 9780804840729 (hardcover)
1. Philippines--Juvenile literature. 2. Philippines--Pictorial works. I. Dandan-Albano, Corazon, 1964- illustrator. II. Title.
DS655.J55 2015
959.9--dc23
                    2015019770

This edition ISBN 978-0-8048-4848-0
(Previously published ISBN 978-0-8048-4072-9)

Distributed by

North America, Latin America & Europe
Tuttle Publishing
364 Innovation Drive
North Clarendon, VT 05759-9436
U.S.A.
Tel: (802) 773-8930
Fax: (802) 773-6993
info@tuttlepublishing.com
www.tuttlepublishing.com

Japan
Tuttle Publishing
Yaekari Building, 3rd Floor
5-4-12 Osaki, Shinagawa-ku
Tokyo 141 0032
Tel: (81) 3 5437-0171
Fax: (81) 3 5437-0755
sales@tuttle.co.jp
www.tuttle.co.jp

Asia Pacific
Berkeley Books Pte. Ltd.
3 Kallang Sector, #04-01
Singapore 349278
Tel: (65) 6741-2178
Fax: (65) 6741-2179
inquiries@periplus.com.sg
www.tuttlepublishing.com

First edition
24 23 22   10 9 8 7 6   2204EP
Printed in China

Contents

Mabuhay! Welcome!

Meet Mary, Jaime and Ari

My name is **Mary Ong**. My skin is pretty fair and I have straight black hair and almond-shaped eyes. I live in Mandaluyong City on Luzon, which is the largest Philippine island. My dad's ancestors were Chinese merchants who first came to the Philippines more than 1000 years ago! My mom is descended from a tribe called Ifugao, who are famous for building the rice terraces in northern Luzon.

Maligayang pagdating!

Malipayong pagabot!

My name is **Jaime Lopez**. I have big round eyes and a pointed nose and light brown hair. I live in Cebu, one of the main islands in Visayas. My dad's ancestors go all the way back to the Spanish explorers that came to this country to claim it as a colony and spread Christianity.

Bienvenidos!

My name is **Ari Abaza**. I have curly black hair and my nose is kind of flat. I live in Zamboanga City on the island of Mindanao, which is where you'll find most of this country's Muslims. My dad is descended from Arab missionaries who came to the Philippines more than 700 years ago.

4

We are cousins.

Our mothers
are sisters.

But we look
very different!

Together, we are a perfect blend, just like the Filipino people.

So many different people make up this country—Malayo-Polynesians, Chinese, South Asian and Arab people who came looking for places to settle and trade. Spanish explorers and American soldiers also came here looking for spices and new lands to conquer.

It's no wonder that our country is known as a land of many different faces, a mix of different sorts of people who are all Filipinos.

Ancestral Voyages

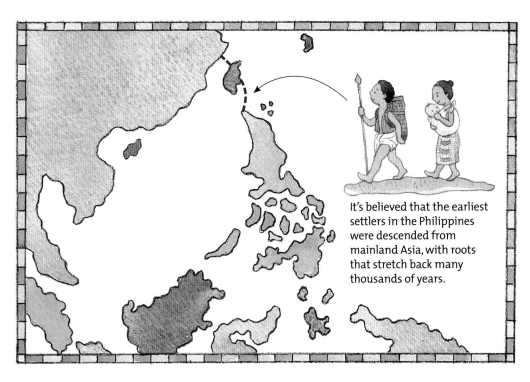

It's believed that the earliest settlers in the Philippines were descended from mainland Asia, with roots that stretch back many thousands of years.

The Philippines is an archipelago, which is a group of islands that form a single country. It is believed that the Philippines's first settlers were descended from mainland Asians who migrated to Taiwan thousands of years ago. Over time, their descendants developed strong seafaring abilities, eventually sailing from Taiwan to the Philippines, Indonesia, Borneo and Malaysia. With so much nautical skill spreading out over the region, trade and migration grew quickly. That's how it all started.

By the 10th century a steady trade route had opened up from India to China. Business boomed. Chinese and Arab traders came to trade exotic new goods and to settle on the islands. They brought new customs, languages and religions to the region.

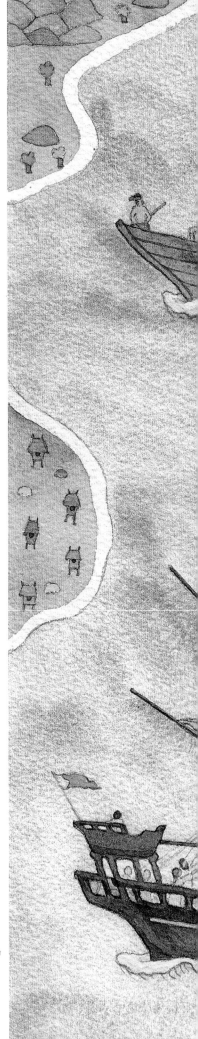

The Barangay Outrigger

A Barangay was a large wooden outrigger that carried the Malayo-Polynesian peoples to the islands. These boats were big enough to carry extended families of a hundred people! The families settled along coasts and riversides all across the islands. The word Barangay now refers to a small community, like a village or neighborhood.

Chinese Junks

Chinese merchants and traders came in their large Junk boats carrying porcelain vases and plates, silks, artillery, incense and tin. Some stayed to create market places where they could sell or trade their goods.

Arab Dhows

Arab traders came in their smaller Dhow boats, bringing with them linens, wool and metal items. Traveling with them were Muslim missionaries who married local women and spread Islam to the people living in the area.

7

Ferdinand Magellan

In 1519, Portuguese explorer Ferdinand Magellan traveled east to find the Spice Islands for Spain. Two years later he sailed with his four remaining carracks onto Philippine shores to replenish supplies in the hopes of finishing his journey.

During their short time on the island of Cebu, Magellan and his men converted many of the island's people to Christianity. But many from the surrounding islands resented these foreign visitors and their Spanish King, Charles I.

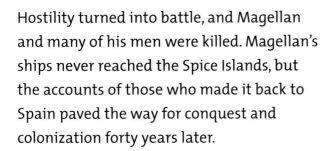

Hostility turned into battle, and Magellan and many of his men were killed. Magellan's ships never reached the Spice Islands, but the accounts of those who made it back to Spain paved the way for conquest and colonization forty years later.

In 1556, the archipelago fell completely under Spanish rule and became known as the Philippines. For 330 years the islands were forced to accept Spain's king, religion and culture as their own. Today, long after Spanish rule, much of Spain's influence is still part of everyday Filipino life.

American Warships

On April 25, 1898, the United States attacked the Spanish stronghold in the capital of Manila. Six small warships easily defeated the entire Spanish fleet. With this victory, control over the Philippines passed to the Americans, who went about educating the Filipinos, teaching them English, developing the land and imposing their style of democratic authority.

General Douglas MacArthur

During World War II the Philippines were invaded and occupied by Japan. In 1945, more American warships, under the command of General Douglas MacArthur, brought the conflict to an end. The Philippines became independent in 1946.

The Philippine Flag

A Story of Philippine Independence

I t all started with a young man named Andres Bonifacio, who formed a secret society known as the Katipunan, which worked for the day that the Philippines would break free of Spanish rule. He created a banner for the society, a simple red flag bearing a KKK that stood for the society's full name: **Ang Kataastaasang Kagalanggalang Katipunan ng mga Anak ng Bayan**, which means "the highest and most venerable society of the children of the country." The red background stood for the blood they were willing to shed and to lose in order to win their freedom.

As the society grew, each of its military leaders created their own red and white flags to carry into battle. Two factions used a sun, and in its center they daringly used a letter that is part of a language that was spoken in pre-Spanish times. Eventually, the letter became the face of the sun.

Sugod, mga Kapatid!!!

Andres Bonifacio

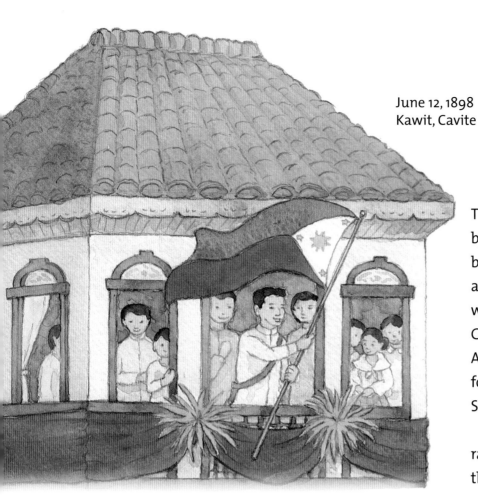

June 12, 1898
Kawit, Cavite

The flag we use today was designed by General Emilio Aguinaldo, who became leader of the KKK society after Andres Bonifacio's death. It was raised on June 12, 1898, when General Aguinaldo, along with the American allies, defeated Spanish forces to finally claim freedom from Spanish rule.

When the country is at war, we raise the flag upside down, so that the red is on top.

The blue on top represents peace, truth and justice.

The white triangle stands for purity and equality.

Inside the triangle, a yellow sun with eight rays symbolizes the first eight provinces that rebelled against Spain.

Three yellow stars on the corners of the triangle stand for the three main island groups Luzon, Visayas and Mindanao.

The red represents patriotism and courage.

Together all these symbols honor the early Filipinos who fought the Spanish colonizers, gaining the independence the Philippines enjoys today.

11

An Earth-Shattering Experience
Basic Geography of the Philippines

There are over 7000 islands making up the Philippines! Less than half of them have names, and only 2000 are large enough to be inhabited.

The Philippine islands spread out over almost 1000 miles of the Southeast Asia region, near Taiwan, Malaysia and Indonesia. If you were to clump the islands into one mass, the country would be about the size of Italy.

Each island is considered part of the Luzon, Visayas or Mindanao group. Nearly all of the islands were formed by volcanoes that originated deep beneath the ocean's floor, and have many mountain ranges, fertile plains, rivers and lakes.

Because the Philippines is just north of the equator its climate is warm and humid most of the year. Being a tropical country, the Philippines has just two seasons--dry and wet! November to May is the dry season, when warm winds called **amihan** travel in a northeast direction. During the wet season cool moist winds called **habagat** move across the islands in a southwest direction, bringing rains. The habagat and amihan are monsoon winds that affect the weather patterns every year. At least twenty powerful storms called **typhoons** form in the Pacific Ocean and pass through the Luzon and Visayas regions. We name our typhoons the same way you name hurricanes in your country.

The dry season—November to May

The wet season—June to October

Let's go island hopping!

1. **Rio Grande de Cagayan** is the longest river in the Philippines.
2. The 2000 year old **Banaue Rice Terraces** were carved into the mountains of Ifugao by the ancestors of the indigenous people.
3. "Rice Bowl of the Philippines" is a nickname given to **Nueva Ecija** for producing most of the country's rice supply.
4. Mary lives near **Fort Santiago**, built by the Spanish conquistador Miguel López de Legazpi in the 1590s.
5. The **Pacific War Memorial** on **Corregidor Island** was a gift from the United States to honor the Philippine soldiers of World War II, and houses many battle relics.
6. **Mayon Volcano** in Albay on the island of Luzon is famous for its nearly perfect cone shape.

7. Guitar crafting is a major art form and industry on Jaime's home island of **Cebu**.
8. The underground river of **Puerto Princesa** was chosen as one of the New Wonders of Nature.
9. The tiny primate the **Philippine Tarsier** is often called "the world's smallest monkey" but is actually from a different primate family.
10. The beautiful **Maria Cristina Falls** generate most of the energy on the island of Mindanao.
11. The **Philippine Eagle** is one of the world's largest eagle species.
12. The **Vinta** is the traditional boat of the **Zamboanga Peninsula** of **Mindanao**, where Ari lives.
13. World-famous boxer Manny Pacquiao was born and raised in **Saranggani**.

Living in a Land of Earthquakes, Volcanoes and Typhoons

Living in the Philippines is an earth-shattering experience! Being the first stop for most tropical storms from the western Pacific Ocean, and with so many faults and volcanoes, the Philippines is more prone to natural disasters than most places on earth.

Would you believe that there are at least five earthquakes happening in different parts of the Philippines every day? An earthquake is what happens when **tectonic plates** rub against each other. A tectonic plate is a broken piece of the earth's crust located under the oceans. These plates are always on the move. The Philippines lies on three very large plates, so you can see why the Philippines have so many earthquakes!

Pacific plate

Philippine plate

Eurasian plate

Australian plate

The Philippines also has 200 volcanoes, and 21 of them are active. Even dormant ones can erupt at any time and cause lots of damage.

But believe it or not, not everything about earthquakes and typhoons and volcanoes is bad. They help make the soil fertile, so the Philippines is rich in crops. They also form beautiful natural attractions like stalactites and stalagmites in Palawan, and coral atolls that rise from the oceans, like the Chocolate Hills of Bohol, and lots more!

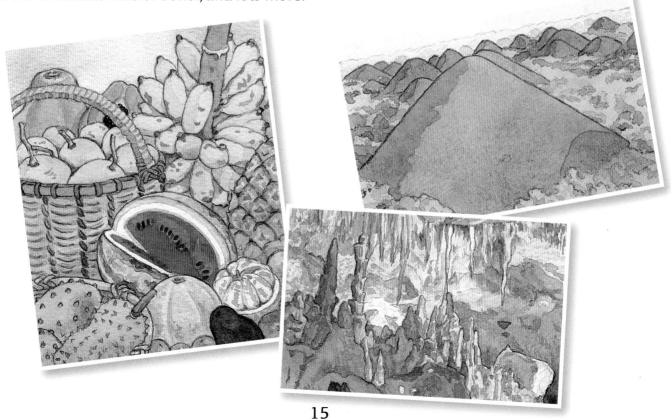

The Case of the Disappearing Rainforests and Coral Reefs

What Happened to the Animals, Plants and Fish?

kalaw

Most of the Philippine islands were once covered with lush forests. The tropical climate—hot temperatures and lots of rainfall—created a great environment for all kinds of plant and animal life.

Since the Philippine islands were isolated from other lands for a long time, many species became *endemic*—unique to the country, like the Philippine Eagle, Tamaraw, Philippine Tarsier and Flying Lemur. About a third of the thousands of plant species and about half of the of bird, mammals and reptile species are unique to these islands. This wildlife has made the Philippine forests one of the most bio-diverse areas in the world.

Bio-diverse (from the words "biological" and "diverse") also describes the enormous coral reef ecosystem located off the Philippine shores. Did you know that, at its healthiest, nearly every known type of coral reef species could be found in the Philippines? Hundreds of marine life species were found only in these reefs.

But with rainforests disappearing and coral reefs dying, the word *endemic* is now being associated with another word—*extinct*—which means no longer living. But who or what is the cause?

Some people feel that this is just the price of progress. Trees were cut down to make houses and boats. Fish were caught to eat or to sell. But in the big rush to use as many of the resources as quickly as possible, practices like mining, illegal logging and dynamite fishing have been killing these ecosystems.

Because the planet can take only so much mistreatment, the seas grew warmer and corals were dying. Seasons became unpredictable, and landslides and floods started destroying habitats—including our own. Case solved, or unresolved?

Traveling Together

Looking for Rice Terraces, Hanging Coffins, Chocolate Hills, the Underground River, and more...

When summer comes around, our families go on trips to see what's happening on other Philippine islands. We only have one rule—never the same island!

A hanging coffin or two?

On our first trip to a place called Sagada in the northern part of Luzon, we wanted to see three things—our grandparents' home, the Banaue rice terraces (they're over 2000 years old!) and the hanging coffins of our maternal ancestors.

Banaue rice terraces

Traditional Ifugao houses

hanging coffins

Our grandparents' home is a concrete bungalow with a thatched roof. But we also got to see traditional Ifugao houses that people lived in when the rice fields were first carved out of the mountains. From these houses, it was easy to spot the hanging coffins of our ancestors. Some of them were shooting out from small caves and nearby cliffs.

Are the hills in Bohol really made of Chocolate?

We could hardly wait to go to the island of Bohol in the central Visayas. We wanted to know if the Chocolate Hills there are really made of chocolate. Of course, it was too good to be true. The hills are only chocolate colored because they are mounds of old coral reef formations that have risen above sea level and have turned brown during the summer.

Exploring the Palawan underground river

We also got to go spelunking (exploring in the caves) of the Puerto Princesa Subterranean River in Palawan, southwest of the Luzon region. We rode in small outrigger boats and saw these beautiful calcium salt formations from the ceiling (stalactites) and the floor (stalagmites). This is one of the longest underground rivers in the world. It was kind of spooky with all the insects and bats along the way, but it was fun!

A Creation Myth

The Story of the Sleeping Giant

There are many myths that explain how the Philippines formed. Here is a popular one about two playful giants playing "hide and seek."

Long ago, before humans roamed the earth, a god named Bathala created a superior race of giants to care for all the living beings on Earth and to protect the environment they lived in. At the end of a hard day's work, the giants liked to get together and have fun. Two young giants named Felipe and Indo usually used this time to play by the sea.

One afternoon, Indo suggested that they play hide-and-seek. Felipe agreed and wanted to hide first. He thought about hiding in the mountains and the forests, but decided it would be too easy to find him in those places because he was so big. He decided to hide in the ocean instead. But since he knew Indo was a good diver, he needed a good camouflage. He put mud all over his body, lay on the ocean floor and didn't move.

When Indo came to look for Felipe, he couldn't find him. Finally, after several attempts, Indo gave up and shouted, "I give up! You win!" But by this time, Felipe could not hear him anymore because he had fallen asleep.

When Indo couldn't find Felipe by nightfall, he told Felipe's parents. All the adult giants went to help find Felipe, shouting, "Felipe! Nasaan ka?" ("Felipe! Where are you?"). Morning came but Felipe was nowhere to be found. Felipe had been having such beautiful dreams that he never woke up.

Soon Bathala called the giants back to his kingdom. They had finished what they were supposed to do on Earth.

The sleeping Felipe was left behind. As time passed, the mud on Felipe's body began to harden. Eventually, living things started to grow on him, such as plants and trees. It wasn't long before the sleeping mound of mud became a string of islands.

Soon a human race of brown-skinned people found the islands and decided to live there. During sunset, the people would faintly hear echoes of voices of the giants still looking for Felipe. But all they could really hear was the phrase "Felipe! Nas...?" Someone thought it might be the name of the islands. "Filipinas!" They thought it was a beautiful name, and from then on they called the islands FILIPINAS.

Languages

A different language for each island people

Filipinos are able to converse in at least two or three different languages. Mary, Jaime, and Ari all speak English, Filipino and a little bit of Ifugao from their moms. But each one of them has a different first language that they speak at home.

At home Mary speaks Fukien Chinese to her dad and grandparents. This is a dialect from southern China. She also learns Mandarin Chinese at school. But she's comfortable speaking in Filipino, since this is the language her parents use when they're talking together.

Jaime's first language is called Cebuano. It's the most widely spoken language in the Central Visayas area.

Ari speaks Chavacano at home. It is a Creole type of Spanish spoken by the locals of Zamboanga City. He is also learning Arabic in his Quran classes at his Islamic school.

Even though they all use different languages at home, the fact that they all speak and write Filipino means that they can always communicate with each other.

Picking a National Language

How can a country as small as the Philippines end up with over 170 different languages and dialects?

Most of the languages spoken in the Philippines came from the Malay Peninsula and Indonesia. The many dialects are regional versions of these languages.

For many years it was hard for the different regions to communicate with each other. Then, in 1397, the country decided to choose a national language. While people would still speak the language of their region, they would learn the national language as well. That way, everyone in the Philippines would be able to understand each other. Tagalog was chosen as the basis for the national language, Filipino.

In 1937, President Manuel Quezon issued a proclamation approving the adoption of a national language.

With both English and Filipino being taught in schools, young people have two languages in common and can easily communicate with each other. But, sadly, because English and Filipino are used so often, some of the regional languages are dying out. To help preserve the regional languages, many schools are teaching all subjects except for English and Filipino in the language that people in the region use at home.

President Manuel L. Quezon

The Language Challenge
Many ways to say **Thank You**

Ilocano

Agyamanak

Inabel
Handwoven cloth
from Ilocos

Because we travel around the country, and so many different languages are spoken here, we've started a language challenge. Everywhere we've visited, people have been friendly and kind. We wanted to learn how to say "thank you" in all of the parts of the country we visit. **Salamat** is the commonly understood word but we've learned other words for "thank you" too, like:

Pis siyabit
A Tausug woven head covering made of silk

Tausug

Magsukul

Thank you!
Salamat!

(Filipino, Pampangan, Pangasinense, Cebuano, Hiligaynon, Waray, Maranao, Ifugao)

Bicol

Mabalos

Pili
Candied pili nuts, a special delicacy from Bicol

There are over 170 ways to say "thank you" in the Philippines. How many can you discover?

Chavacano

Gracias

Maguindanao

Sukran

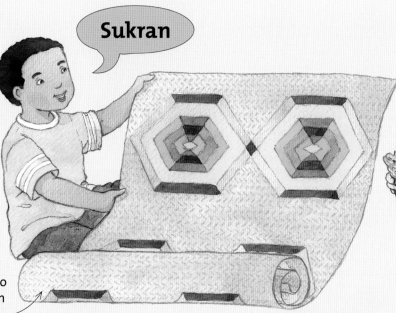

Ekam
A colorful Maguindanao mat made from pandan leaves

Lokot-lokot
A delicacy from Zamboanga made from rice

Not Your Everyday Filipino

The Barong Tagalog

Jaime wears a **barong tagalog** on special occasions. The barong is a Philippine national costume for men. It is made from a delicate fabric called **piña** that is handwoven from pineapple fiber.

   It is commonly believed that the barong may have originated as a uniform for Filipinos during Spanish colonial times. The shirt's see-through material and tucked-out design with no pockets prevented the wearer from stealing or hiding weapons.

The Jeepney

When Mary misses her school bus, she takes a **jeepney** to school. A jeepney is a public mode of transportation that looks kind of like a colorful army jeep. After the American occupation, many surplus jeeps were left behind and converted for commercial use. Jeepneys are decorated according to the owners' personal tastes, and each is unique. Many owners paint pictures of their family and religious icons, like Jesus, on their jeepney.

Kulintang
an ancient musical instrument composed of metal gongs

Dabakan
a Maranao drum

The Singkil and Tinikling

Ari and his friends love clapping bamboo poles for a popular Muslim dance called the **singkil**, named after the bells worn on the dancers' ankles. In this dance, two sets of poles are criss-crossed and placed an equal and suitable distance apart. The dance is based on a legend about a Muslim princess who gets lost in a forest during an earthquake caused by mischievous fairies. Ari's school teaches the singkil as part of Philippine culture, and many real-life Muslim princesses still perform the dance during important royal functions.

The **tinikling** is another dance that uses poles. This Luzon folk dance is believed to have originated as a form of punishment in the Spanish haciendas. Slow workers would be made to stand between two poles. If they didn't want the poles to strike their ankles, they'd have to jump out of the way. The dainty steps of this dance mimic the movements of the **tikling** (heron), a local bird considered a nuisance in the fields.

pawid
nipa

Bahay Kubo
Nipa hut

Bayanihan
A tradition that involves working together to lift and move a house to a new location

kawayan
bamboo

The Bahay Kubo

Is it really possible to pick up an entire house and move it to a different location in a single day? In the Philippines, counting on the Filipino community spirit of **bayanihan** can be a common occurrence, especially with the threat of flood during the typhoon season. The old town tradition involves all able-bodied men coming together to carry the house to a new location.

A **bahay kubo** is a cube-shaped house made from local natural materials of bamboo and nipa. It is built on wooden stilts as a protective measure against unwanted wild animals. It is also easier to uproot when the house needs to be transported to another location.

A popular song called "Bahay Kubo" describes a peaceful, abundant and contented life in this simple little house.

Bahay Kubo (Filipino)

Ba- hay Ku- bo, ka- hit mun- ti Ang ha- la- man do-

on ay — sa- ri sa- ri Singka mis at ta- long, siga

ri-lyas at ma- ni, Sit- aw bat- aw pa- ta- ni.

Nipa Hut (English)

Nipa hut, even though it is small
The plants it houses are varied
Turnip and eggplant, winged bean and peanut
String bean, hyacinth bean, lima bean.

Wax gourd, luffa, white squash and pumpkin,
And there is also radish, mustard,
Onion, tomato, garlic and ginger
And all around are sesame seeds.

The **Malacanang Palace** in Manila is the seat of the Philippine National Government, just like the White House is in the U.S.

Growing up in Luzon

The main island of Luzon is my home. It is the largest and most populated island in the Philippines. It's also home to the largest number of ethnic groups in the country. Lots of the people here are of Austronesian or Malayo-Polynesian descent, like my mother's Ifugao tribe. Some people are descended from minority immigrants who came to trade and then settled in Manila, like my father's Chinese ancestors.

A lot of Luzon's population live in Metro Manila, which is a group of cities that has been the center of government and business since colonial times. People who live here come from many different places, but most of the people here speak Tagalog or Filipino and English. Most of them are Roman Catholics.

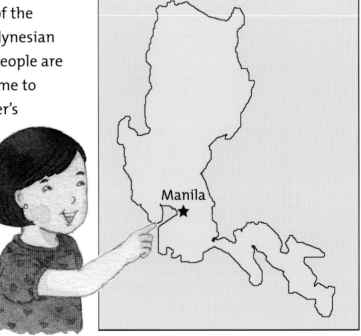

Manila

My parents and I live in Mandaluyong city, one of the sixteen cities that make up Metro Manila. We live in a three-story town house with my grandparents. We moved here from Binondo, the original Chinatown of Manila, so we could live closer to the private Chinese Catholic school that my parents picked for me. Lots of my schoolmates' families moved to this area for its schools. Now our neighborhood is a kind of Chinatown, with lots of fantastic Chinese shops and restaurants.

The monument of our national hero Jose Rizal in Luneta. Rizal was a doctor and writer who advocated reform by peaceful means, and worked for equal treatment of Filipinos when the Philippines was a colony of Spain. His portrait has appeared on much of our currency.

Mary's Everyday World

Every morning I wake up to the smell of simmering spices from food being cooked for my grandparents' food shop. My **Yaya** (Nanny) Helen comes into my room with a freshly ironed school uniform at exactly 6:15 and nudges me out of bed. She hurries me to eat breakfast with my parents before they go to work.

My parents are both accountants at different banks in Makati, the financial district of Metro Manila. Since they work full time, they hired Yaya Helen to help take care of me. I kiss my mom and dad on the cheek and sit down to our breakfast of congee (rice porridge) with all kinds of great toppings. My favorite is pork floss (shredded sweetened dried pork).

After breakfast, my parents drop me and my Yaya at a stop along the road where my school bus stops to pick me up. Other girls who live nearby wait there, too, and board the bus with me. It takes only fifteen minutes for us to get to school.

lugaw
congee

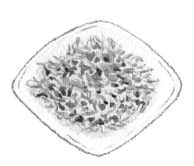

pork floss

School starts at exactly 7:15 every morning and ends at 3:00 in the afternoon. This is my first year in high school. All my classes are taught in English and Filipino, except for my Mandarin language class. Since my dad's family speaks Fukien, another Chinese dialect, I have to take extra lessons from a tutor after school to help me with my Mandarin.

When I get home, my **Ah ma** (grandmother) calls me to the kitchen of her food shop and lets me choose something for **merienda** (afternoon snack). She likes to make me guess the ingredients in the food I eat. She is teaching me some of her secret family recipes. I inherited my love of cooking from Ah ma. Maybe someday I'll have a food shop myself.

Siomai
Steamed pork dumplings

Growing up in the Visayas

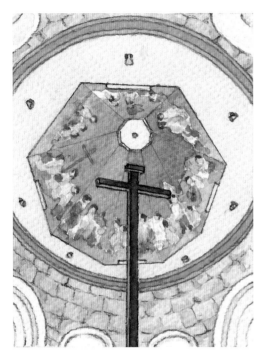

One of the most important landmarks on our island is the cross that Portuguese explorer Ferdinand Magellan planted here to show that Christianity had come to the country.

My family and I live on the island of Cebu. Like other smaller islands in the Visayas, Cebu is known for beautiful beaches, and for one of the Philippines' best exports—mangoes!

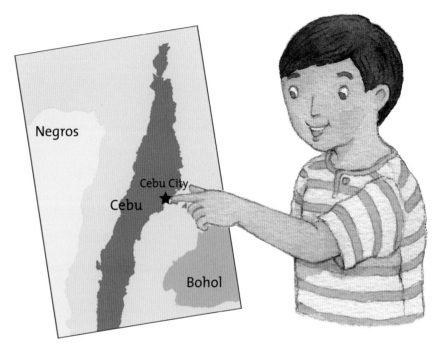

My family is a **mestizo** (mixed) blend of both early Spanish and Malay settlers who came to the islands from nearby Asian countries. We speak a local dialect called Cebuano and are Roman Catholics.

We have a small three-bedroom bungalow on the outskirts of Cebu City. It is one of six houses near my grandparents' house. They had a house built for each of their children. It is nice to have so many of my cousins close by. The large compound that we live on also contains our family's mango plantation and factory for processing dried mangoes.

My dad and his five siblings all work in the family business. Even my cousins and I help out when we can. During the summer months of April or May, when we harvest mangoes, we all help pick them while they are still green. Then they are specially ripened before they are processed and dried. Dried mangos are delicious! We sell them to the leading local grocery and tourist centers. Some of our dried mangos are exported to countries like Japan and Italy.

I don't have to wait for mangoes to ripen before eating them. I eat them with a shrimp paste called **bagoong**. It smells very fishy but it makes the mangoes taste terrific—sweet and tart at the same time!

Green mango
with **bagoong**

33

I always start my day with a heavy breakfast. A dish my mom often makes for my little sister and me is rice with **danggit** (fried crispy fish) and scrambled eggs.

danggit
fried crispy dried fish

Jaime's Everyday World

After breakfast, I go to my cousin's house. She and I go to the same high school, so we usually walk to school together instead of taking the tricycle like my sister and younger cousins. Since the roads in our neighborhood are small, tricycles are the most common form of public transportation. On rainy days I go with my sister. But on sunny days, my cousin and I don't mind the short walk, as we love seeing the rolling waves along the coast.

Almost all my classmates speak only Cebuano at home, but our classes are taught in English and Filipino. My mom grew up as

34

an Ifugao in the northern Luzon mountains, but she went to university in Manila, where she met my dad. I am lucky that mom taught me how to speak all three languages when I was really little. I inherited my love of learning from my mom so I never really have any problems in school.

From my dad, I inherited my love of music. We sometimes go to my friend's family's guitar shop after school. The art of making guitars is another Spanish legacy the friars left in Cebu. Guitar making is always going on in the shop, so there is always a master tuner ready to test a new guitar with us and teach us a song or two.

On the way home, if we still have time, we borrow skimboards from some of the small resorts by the beach. Skimboards are smaller and thinner than surfboards, and you use them to ride out to the waves on that shallow bit of water the surf leaves behind, and back to the beach. Most resorts lend them to local kids like us because it encourages the tourists.

35

Taluksangay
Mosque

Growing up in Mindanao

My father's ancestors were Badjaos, the original sea gypsies of Mindanao. They used to live on small sailboats called **vintas** and got everything they needed from the sea.

Our family doesn't live on a vinta. We live in a nice, simple two-story concrete house in the middle of Zamboanga City. But the sea and the vinta are still very much a part of our lives.

Zamboanga City

Like many men in the city, my father is a fisherman. He fishes for tuna and sardines and sells them in restaurants and factories where they are put in cans.

My mother has a stall at the famous barter market. She sells colorful **malongs** (traditional Muslim wrap-around skirts) and mats made by local women from nearby islands. Though people now pay money instead of trading goods, one practice still happens all the time at the barter market—bargaining for the best price. The common language used for haggling by most Zamboanguenos is Chavacano, a Creole type of Spanish that was adapted by both Muslims and Christians who live in the city. Zamboanga was the only place in Mindanao where Spanish colonizers could establish a fort, and they influenced the local language and converted some residents to Christianity.

Every year it is a source of pride for my father's family to enter a vinta in the annual Regatta at the Hermosa Festival. Everyone in the family helps. My mom asks her supplier of mats to make a colorful sail for the vinta. My dad and his brothers take turns entering the annual race. This year my older cousin and I were asked to start training with our fathers so that we can continue the tradition someday.

Ari's Everyday World

A prayer rug

The very first thing my family does every morning is pray. As Muslims, we are required to pray five times a day. My dad taught us that wherever we are, we must pray in the direction of Mecca, the birthplace of the Prophet Muhammad. We hear prayers being broadcast from the loudspeaker of a nearby mosque while we say our morning prayers. There are many mosques in Zamboanga.

I go to an Islamic school with my two younger brothers just like my older sister and my father did. My sister lives in Manila now, finishing up her studies at the University of the Philippines.

The Quran (Koran)

In school, we learn all the basic subjects taught in Philippine schools, but we also learn the teachings of Quran, the main religious text of Islam.

My dad says it's important that we understand our faith so we can practice it wherever we are and wherever life takes us. My mom was a Christian but she converted to Islam when she married my dad.

Most days after school, my friends and I go to the neighborhood court to shoot some basketball hoops. A few days a week, I stay after school to learn to play the **kulintang**, a brass percussion instrument that's part of a gong ensemble. My sister is getting married at the end of the year and my parents have asked me to perform the kulintang during her wedding ceremony!

Games We Play Together

The Filipino word for "play" is **laro**. When Filipino kids say **laro tayo!** (let's play!), we can do it without needing toys or games.

We like video games and board games and other toys. We like all sorts of sports, too. But sometimes when our families took summer trips together we didn't have any of these things handy—not even a ball or hoops to shoot baskets. And guess what! We still had a great time! Here are a few of the games we love.

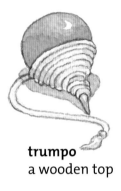

trumpo
a wooden top

taka
a papier mache
toy horse

palayok-palayokan
a mini clay pot

Sipa

Sipa means to kick. This game is sort of like Footbag or "Hacky Sack" in that it involves kicking an object to keep it off the ground for as long as you can. In the traditional version, it involves two teams of four men each who kick a rattan ball back and forth across a net on a court. This ancient game is also called **sepak takraw**. In the street version, kids kick a covered metal washer up in the air as many times as they can until it falls to the ground. The player who kicks the washer the most number of times wins.

Rattan ball

1	2
3	4
5	6

Patintero

Pick two teams of five players each. The object of the game is to get the members of your team across to a home base protected by the opposing team. Each team takes turns running to their respective bases. All the members of a team are strategically positioned so as to keep their opponents from passing. Once a person is tagged as they are trying to reach the base, they are considered out of the game.

How to make your own *Sipa*

It is easy to make your own sipa. You can find many of the materials that you will need in your local hardware store.

What you will need:

1 metal washer (1" or 2 cm)
Flat straw rope
Ruler
Scissors
Glue

How to make it:

1. Measure and cut 6-8 pieces of rope into 1-foot lengths.
2. Fold the rope pieces in half until all the edges are even.
3. Make a knot at the looped end of the rope pieces.
4. Pull the ends through the hole of the washer until the knot is wedged.
5. You can apply glue where the knot meets the washer to hold it securely in place.

pamato
flat stones
or coins

Piko

Piko is a Filipino version of the American game hopscotch. A player hops on a diagram shaped like a **bahay kubo** (nipa hut). Players take turns throwing flat stones onto the boxes making up the house as they hop up and down. When the player is able to jump up and down the house without stepping on the lines, he or she gets a house point. The player with the most house points wins.

Sungka

For this game you need two players and a **sungkaan**, a long oblong-shaped wooden block. The sungkaan has two rows of seven circular holes on each side and two larger holes on either end. You can use shells, pebbles or seeds as game pieces. The object of the game is to try to make as many game pieces as you can land on your side of the block. The player who collects the most number of game pieces wins the game. Though a sungkaan is very bulky, we always try to bring one along on family trips. **Sungka** was a favorite game our moms used to play, especially when they were growing up and had nothing to do during the rainy season.

mga paka
shells

Why Can't You Take a Bath on Good Friday?

In the Philippines, holidays like Chinese New Year, Holy Week, All Saint's Day, Eid'l Fitr and Christmas are special times when families celebrate traditions and beliefs handed down from generation to generation.

Mary - Chinese New Year

Although we celebrate the coming of the Western new year like the rest of the country, we also celebrate Chinese New Year in late January or early February.

We spend the new year with our relatives who live in Binondo, where there is always a big celebration. We greet our elders "kiong hee huat choi," which means "may your life be prosperous" in our Fukien dialect. In return, they give us red envelopes called **angpao** with crisp **peso** bills in them.

We go out to the streets and make our own loud noise with the dragon dance parade. We also enjoy the fireworks display put together as an annual community event. Both are traditions to drive away evil and are meant to bring good luck for the new year.

angpao
red envelopes

44

Jaime - Holy Week

For forty days leading up to Easter Sunday, Christians observe a period called Lent, when we remember the sacrifice our Lord Jesus Christ made by dying for our sins.

During Lent we make our own sacrifices by giving up certain things such as meat, or sweets, or video games.

abo
ash

mga palaspas
palm leaves

Forty days before Easter, on a day called Ash Wednesday, we put ash cross marks on our foreheads to symbolize the start of the period of fasting and repentance. We visit many churches and pray about Jesus' suffering. We bless palm leaves to ward off evil spirits. The Friday before Easter Sunday is called Good Friday and it is the day that Jesus died. It's a Filipino tradition not to take a bath on Good Friday because of an old belief that it could make you sick.

On Easter Sunday, we celebrate Jesus's resurrection from the dead by going to mass—and, afterwards, finally getting to eat all the things we gave up during Lent.

Mary - Undas (All Saint's Day) (November 1st)

On the evening of October 31st, my grandmother closes her food shop early to make all the favorite foods of her departed parents and in-laws. I go to sleep knowing that she will wake us up early to go to the Manila Chinese Cemetery, where we will remember and pray for our relatives who have passed away.

November 1st, also called **Undas**, is a day when most Filipinos pay their respects to their loved ones who have died. Most bring flowers, candles, and food to the cemeteries. Some people stay all day and have family reunions there. The cemetery is usually solemn place, but on this day it becomes festive, with pitched tents, loud music, and food vendors.

We Chinese bring food not only for ourselves but as offerings for the dead in the afterlife as well. We also burn offerings of paper money for their needs in the afterlife.

Ari - Eid'l Fitr (End of Ramadan)

Eid'l Fitr is the celebration of the end of the holy month of Ramadan. It is held on the 10th month of the Islamic year. During the thirty days of Ramadan, Muslim families like mine observe **puasa** (fasting). We are only allowed to take a light meal before the sun rises every morning and then a heavy meal after the sun sets. We are also expected to be on our best behavior during this time.

On the morning of **Eid'l Fitr**, the day we break our fast, we all do a ritual cleaning of our house. Then we ask each other for forgiveness. We go to a religious service in the mosque and celebrate afterwards with lots of spicy food, and even presents!

Simbang Gabi

Parol
a Christmas lantern

Christmas (December 25th)

December 16th is the official start of the Christmas season for Filipino Christians. It is the start of **simbang gabi** (night mass), when some people go to mass every day at dawn for nine days, in the hope of getting a prayer or wish answered.

Namamasko Po!
Along with Christmas gifts, children show respect to elders and receive their blessings for the coming year.

Noche Buena is what we call the traditional meal we enjoy after Midnight Mass. It includes foods like the ham many westerners enjoy at Christmas dinner, and **Queso de Bola**—a ball of Edam cheese—as well fruit salad and other yummy dishes.

Make a simple parol!

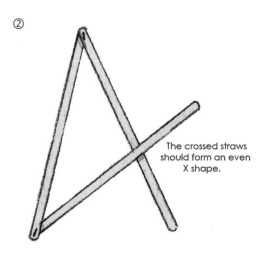

If you wake up early enough to attend **simbang gabi**, you'll see colorful **parols** hanging in many front windows. In Filipino homes, moms hang up the homemade ones their kids have made. In Spanish colonial times, these parols would light the way for mass goers as they went to church in the dark.

This type of parol doesn't hold a candle, but it still catches the spirit of the holiday.

You'll need:

5 straws
A small stapler
A 6-8" length of ribbon or yarn for hanging

For the streamers you'll need:

Tissue paper cut into about four thin strips (or any even number of strips, depending on how many strands you'd like your streamers to have), about 8-10 inches long

①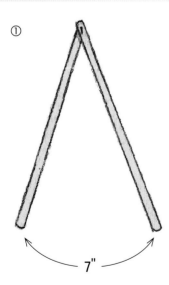

7"

②

The crossed straws should form an even X shape.

1. Staple two straws at the tips, as shown in diagram 1, making sure the bottom ends are about 7 inches apart. This gives you an inverted V-shape

2. With another straw, make a new point at the lower left end of your V, as shown in diagram 2. Make sure your straw is placed at a good angle before stapling in place.

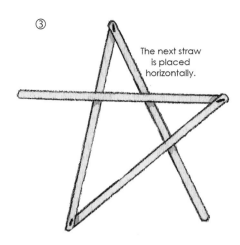

③ The next straw is placed horizontally.

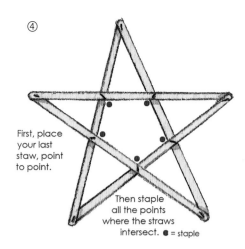

④ First, place your last staw, point to point.

Then staple all the points where the straws intersect. ● = staple

3. Following diagrams 3 and 4, staple the last two points in place with your two remaining straws.

4. When all the points of the star are stapled, staple at all the other places where straws touch each other (see diagram 4).

5. Now it's time to add streamers. You can add them to the two lower points, the two side points, or all four. Two strips of paper folded in half lengthwise will give you four streamers. Staple your folded strips to the points. If you like, you can gently knot your strips together at the middle before stapling. You can also use yarn or ribbon to make streamers, as long as they are not too heavy for the straws.

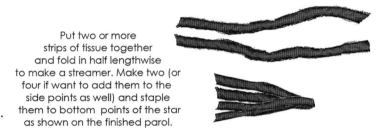

Put two or more strips of tissue together and fold in half lengthwise to make a streamer. Make two (or four if want to add them to the side points as well) and staple them to bottom points of the star as shown on the finished parol.

6. Loop your ribbon or yarn through the top point and tie so you can hang your parol .

This fast and easy parol is just one way to do it. You can also make the sides of a parol using strips of cardboard (the cardboard from a cereal box is a good thickness) or thin strips of wood. Glue the points in place or fasten with string or rubber bands. Decorate the star with paint or glitter. Cut brightly colored tissue paper to fit the points and center of the star and use a glue stick to apply the cut pieces to the sides of the star (be gentle—tissue paper tears easily). Make streamers with crepe paper, strips of fabric, or ribbon. When you think about it, you can make a fantastic parol just with things you already have at home! Have fun!

Family First!

Family always comes first for Filipinos. It is not unusual for Filipino families to have three generations living under one roof—grandparents, parents and their kids ! In addition to looking after their spouses and kids, adults often take care of their elders and even their younger brothers and sisters. And everyone in the family helps out.

Lots of people live at home until they get married. Sometimes, they never leave, staying to take care of their elderly parents. This Filipino trait is called **utang na loob**, which means "a debt of one's self"—giving back to our parents in gratitude to them for caring for us when we were kids.

tito
Uncle

tatay
Father

anak
Child

kuya
Older brother

pinsan
Cousin

lolo
Grandfather

To show respect to older family members, we usually say hello by either giving them a kiss on the cheek or by touching the back of their hand to our forehead. This custom is called **pagmamano**. We say **mano po**, which means "hands please," to respectfully ask their permission to greet them.

It is considered impolite to call someone older than you by their first name.

Most of our regional dialects have words that make what we say sound more formal and polite. In Filipino, we say **ho** and **po** when talking to our elders to show our respect.

Here are some of the respectful terms we commonly use in Filipino:

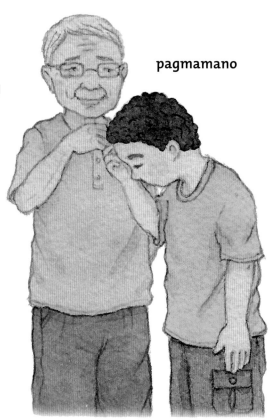

pagmamano

nanay
Mother

tita
Aunt

ate
Older sister

lola
Grandmother

51

Fiesta!

Almost every Filipino **barrio** (town) has a fiesta at least once a year. Many of them started out as simple thanksgiving celebrations after a good harvest. Farmers would offer some of their best fruits and vegetables to **Anitos** (Earth Gods) to thank them for their blessings. Prayers were said to ask for protection over the next harvest.

palay · durian · buko · saging · marang · mabolo · duhat · mangga · mangosteen

Poon
a statue

Long ago, celebrations were pretty simple, but when the Spanish colonized here celebrations became lively, colorful fiestas with lots of food, games and contests. While the Filipino still held festivals to pray for a good harvest, they also found other reasons to celebrate, many to do with their new Roman Catholic religion and new Christian God.

Today, many fiestas still revolve around Christian rituals. Masses and processions of people carrying images of Jesus Christ or statues of Christian saints are held throughout the day. This is also the time when the townspeople show off their best produce and cook special local dishes for visiting relatives and friends. That is why our families love going to different places in the country—to attend the fiestas!

The Pahiyas Festival (Lucban, Quezon)

One of our favorite fiestas in northern Luzon is the Pahiyas festival, known for its colorful rice wafers called **kiping**. It is celebrated every 15th of May. The residents prepare a long time for this day by decorating their houses with homemade kiping and other local produce, such as native **sinamay** hats, vegetables and fruits.

We walked through the town in a procession to honor the Catholic saint San Isidro Labrador, the patron saint of farmers. At the end of the day, the house with the best decorations wins a prize. This announcement also signals the best part of the day—when we get to pick and eat all the decorations of the houses.

sinamay hat

kiping
colorful rice wafer

The Sinulog Festival (Cebu)

Although the Sinulog has only been part of the festival scene since 1980, it has become one of the most popular fiestas in Central Visayas. One reason for that is that everyone loves dancing to loud drums and gongs in the streets of Cebu during the Grand Parade. The Sinulog dance—named after the Cebuano word for "water current"—is supposed to resemble the current of Cebu's Pahina River. The steps are easy—two steps forward and one step backward.

Originally a pagan dance to wooden idols representing the Anitos (spirits), the Sinulog was adopted as a simple dance ritual by candle vendors in the Basilica Minore del Santo Niño. Over time it evolved into the huge celebration it is today. It commemorates the time when Magellan gave an image of Santo Niño—the Holy Child—to the wife of the Rajah upon her baptism. It is celebrated every third Sunday of January.

The Hermosa Festival (Zamboanga)

The Hermosa Festival is celebrated in Zamboanga City every October 12th. It is also known as the Fiesta Pilar, the feast day of Nuestra Senora la Virgen del Pilar (Our Lady of the Pilar, the name given to the virgin mother of Jesus Christ), the patron saint of the city. She serves as a unifying symbol in the only city where the Spanish were able to establish a colonial presence in the South, which is mostly Islamic. She is a legendary protector of the whole city.

Prayers are offered to her image at her shrine at Fort Pilar, and a procession is held to carry her statue all over town. Her feast day is celebrated with unique Zamboangan cultural traditions such as the Vinta Regatta. Ari's family always enters a family boat into the regatta. When we attended the festival, we all got to ride their family vinta before it joined the rest of the entries at the starting line.

prusisyon
a procession

The Perfect Fiesta Table

One of the best things about a fiesta is the food. This is the time of year when Filipinos show off their best dishes. Some of these are only served once a year because they take a lot of time and ingredients to prepare. Most of them are special because they come from family recipes handed down from generation to generation from our colorful mix of ancestors.

Although we think most fiesta foods are yummy, we have our own favorites. Here are the ones we think would make a perfect fiesta table:

kare-kare

menudo

pakwan

bagoong

relyeno

chopsuey

kaldereta

barbecue

crispy pata

leche flan

Mary's Picks

Pancit – a stir-fried egg noodle dish introduced by the first Filipino Chinese immigrants in noodle houses called panciterias. Since then, different regions have made their own kind of pancit using different noodles and sauces with local ingredients. My two favorites are the **pancit malabon**—with its fat, round, white noodles and orange-colored seafood-flavored sauce sprinkled with crunchy bits of pork rind—and the bihon noodle my Ah ma makes for me on my birthday, with thin white rice noodles, peanuts and Chinese sausage to wish me a long life.

PANCIT BIHON

sitsaro
green bean

hipon
shrimp

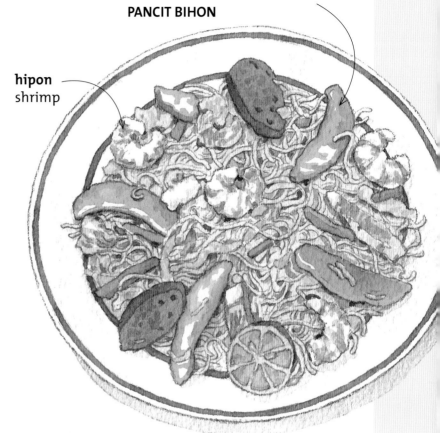

LUMPIANG SHANGHAI

sawsawan
dip

letsugas
lettuce

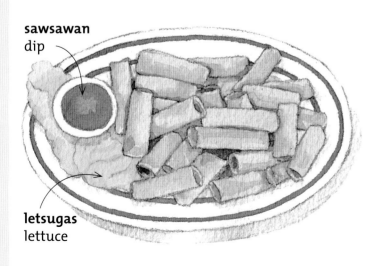

Lumpia – a Filipino version of a spring roll with minced ground pork and vegetables wrapped in either flour- or egg-based wrappers. The original version was sold on the streets by old Chinese women vendors and prepared fresh in the cart. The kind I like is called lumpiang shanghai. I like it better than the fresh ones because they are very crunchy. They are not as healthy because they are fried in lots of oil, but they are very tasty, especially with a sweet and sour dipping sauce.

Jaime's Picks

Though **lechon** is the Spanish term for "pig," versions of this dish are also found in many other Asian countries, so it probably comes from East Asia. The mark of a good lechon is the crispiness of the skin. Following Filipino custom, it is polite not to take too much skin. My elders tell me that if you help yourself to too much skin, you may not be invited back again. My favorite part of the lechon is the ribs.

LECHON
ROASTED PIG

dahon ng saging
banana leaf

sarsa
sauce

mansanas
apple

Halo-Halo —an ice dessert we eat during summer fiestas. It is such a fun dessert because you can pick and choose what you want to put in, like different sweetened beans, preserved fruits, colored tapioca balls, jello, custard and even ice cream. You can even add milk and sugar to make it creamier and sweeter. Then you mix it all together! That's why it's called Halo-Halo, which means "mix-mix."

Ari's Picks

Filipino Barbecue (BBQ) – bite-sized barbecued pork or chicken skewered on thin bamboo sticks cooked with a sweet and salty sauce. A fiesta in any region is never complete without the smoke and smell of charcoal-grilled BBQ nearby!

In Zamboanga where I live, we serve **satti**, a sweet and spicy variety of chicken BBQ. There are many Muslims like me who do not eat pork because of our religious beliefs.

Polvoron – a candy made during the American occupation from pow-dered milk brought in by the Americans. Though it has the same name as a Spanish shortbread, it tastes and looks nothing like its namesake. No baking is required for this unique Filipino dessert—you just have to fry all the ingredients together and mold them into candies. Polvorons are often used in fiestas during whistling contests. Try whistling with a whole polvoron in your mouth! It's not that easy.

This is a perfect treat when you want something that's just a little sweet. And it's really easy to make! (You'll need to use the stove, so be sure to get your parents' permission and supervision.)

You'll need:

3 ½ cups sifted flour
2 ½ cups powdered milk
1 ½ cups granulated sugar
1 cup melted butter
food wrapping paper, like
   parchment or cupcake paper
polvoron molds, candy molds, or
   fun-shaped ice molds

How to make it:

1. Toast flour in a pan over medium heat until slightly brown. Stir constantly to prevent flour from sticking to the pan.
2. Combine the toasted flour, milk, sugar and butter with a wooden spoon.
3. Pack the powdered mixture into polvoron molds. Small candy molds or soft plastic ice trays—the kind that make fun shapes—can be used instead.
4. Release the newly formed candies from the molds and wrap in food wrapping paper. (When using ice or candy molds, pop the filled molds in the freezer for a few minutes first. The coldness will help keep the povorons from breaking as you release them).

Pancit

A Filipino birthday celebration is never complete without **pancit** (a noodle dish) to signify long life. **Pancit bihon guisado**, a family favorite, is made with rice sticks and an assortment of preferred meats and seasonally available vegetables. Here's an easy, yummy recipe.

You need to cut and chop ingredients, and use the stove, so be sure to get your parents' permission and supervision.

You'll need:

8 ounces rice noodles (from the Asian section of your grocery store)
½ pound medium-sized shrimp (peeled and deveined)
1 piece chicken breast (boiled and shredded)
1 small onion (peeled and sliced)
3 cloves garlic (crushed and minced)

¼ green cabbage (shredded in ½ inch pieces)
1 small carrot (peeled and sliced)
2 cups chicken broth
3 tablespoons soy sauce
Salt and pepper to taste
Scallions (chopped for garnish)
Lime (slices for garnish)

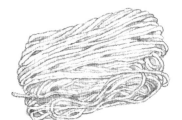
rice noodles

shrimp

green cabbage

scallions

How to make it:

1. Check the noodle package for any special directions. Soak the noodles if so directed.
2. Heat the oil in a large saucepan. Saute the onion and garlic.
3. Add the chicken and shrimp. When the shrimp turns pink, add the cabbage and carrots. Stir fry for a few minutes until the vegetables are slightly tender. Set aside the chicken, shrimp and vegetable mixture.
4. Pour the chicken broth into the pan and add the rice noodles and soy sauce. Boil the noodles until about ¾ of the broth has been absorbed. Add the chicken, shrimp and vegetable mixture back to noodles.
5. Mix and fry everything until all the liquid has been evaporated. Add salt and pepper as needed. Garnish with chopped scallions and sliced limes.

soy sauce

Halo-halo

This refreshing sweet treat is literally named after the way it is made. Halo means to mix. It is fun to mix together a colorful assortment of sweetened fruits and beans topped with heaps of shaved ice, milk and sugar to beat the heat. For an extra special treat, you can add custard or ice cream to the already heaping layers of ice and sweets.

   This is a traditional recipe. Although most of the ingredients are available in Asian food stores as bottled preserved sweets, you can also improvise if some ingredients aren't available. (It won't be quite as Filipino, but it'll still be sweet and fun!)

You'll need:

Sweetened beans—garbanzos, white beans (or you can substitute a fruit, or Pinipig (pounded crushed young rice) for one of these kinds of beans) and kidney beans
Sweetened fruits (plantain bananas, sweet potatoes)
Nata de coco (preserved coconut gel cubes)
Macapuno (preserved coconut strips)

Gulaman (colorful cubed local jello)
Sago (cooked tapioca pearls)
Leche flan (caramel custard)
Ube halaya (purple yam jam)
Evaporated milk
White sugar
Shaved ice
Ice cream or custard

How to make it:

Use a tall parfait glass to layer all the ingredients one by one. It is topped off with crushed ice. Sugar and milk are added upon serving. You can use as much or as little of an ingredient as you like!

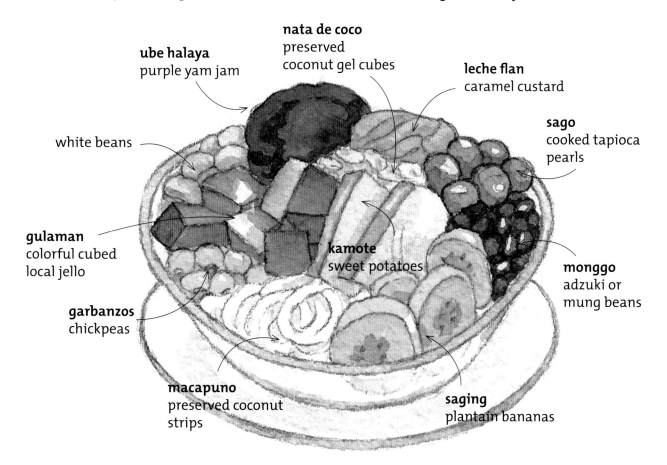

ube halaya
purple yam jam

nata de coco
preserved
coconut gel cubes

leche flan
caramel custard

sago
cooked tapioca
pearls

white beans

kamote
sweet potatoes

monggo
adzuki or
mung beans

gulaman
colorful cubed
local jello

garbanzos
chickpeas

macapuno
preserved coconut
strips

saging
plantain bananas

A Royal Reunion

Aside from holidays and fiestas, weddings are another reason for a family reunion. My sister Aliyah is getting married to Nur, who belongs to a long line of Filipino Muslim royalty. Jaime's and Mary's families are coming. I can't wait! It will be the first royal Muslim wedding for all of us. It'll be really different from the many Christian weddings we've all attended before.

Unlike in Roman Catholic weddings that take place with priests in churches, Aliyah and Nur's marriage rituals will take place at both their houses with the help of an **Imam**, a Muslim religious leader.

On the day of the ceremony, the bride first stays in a private room with her bridesmaids, away from her groom. In a ritual called **wali**, a representative of the groom will sing or chant a public request to open the door to where the bride is waiting. When the bride gives a ring to the groomsman, she is letting him know that her door can be opened. The Imam then leads the groom into her room and the formal ceremony, called **pagkawin**, can begin.

On one of the days before the ceremony, Nur's family came to our house to give my sister a dowry of gifts called **mahr**. He gave her some beautiful jewelry that's been in his family for many years, and some rich fabric she can use for her formal traditional Muslim clothing. The mahr is supposed to symbolize Nur's ability to provide for her. This is like the tradition of **pamanhikan** in Filipino Christian families, which is when the bride and groom officially get engaged.

The day before the wedding, a group of ladies from the bride's family give her advice about what to expect from marriage and family life in a ritual called **bi-at**. This is a little like the bridal shower that women have before Christian weddings. I guess this is one of those traditions where it doesn't matter what your religion is!

As part of the pagkawin, Nur will sit down with elders and the Imam to hear their advice for a good marriage.

During the pagkawin, it's customary for the groom to touch the bride's forehead while saying a prayer for her and for blessing in the marriage.

The bride and groom are presented to the bride's guests, and the groom takes his bride to his house to introduce her to his whole family. Then they go back to the bride's house to celebrate. There will be a huge feast with lots of delicious food, of course!

My parents have asked my brothers and me to play the gong and kulintang with our teachers from our Madrasah Islam school. We will be wearing traditional formal Muslim dress. My mom also put together some formal malongs for Mary's and Jaime's families to wear. We are all so excited to dress up for this royal wedding!

I wish the wedding day would hurry up and come! We're going to have the best time ever! Isn't it great that we can all celebrate together, even though we all have different beliefs, and different customs at home? That's because we are family! That's because we are Filipino!

Index

Here are some great websites for further exploration of the Philippines!

Infoplease www.infoplease.com/country/philippines.html
National Commission for Culture and the Arts https://ncca.gov.ph
National Geographic Kids http://kids.nationalgeographic.com/explore/countries/philippines/
National Museum of the Philippines www.nationalmuseum.gov.ph
Philippines—UNESCO World Heritage Centre http://whc.unesco.org/en/statesparties/ph